WHY GOD USED
D.L. MOODY

WHY **GOD** USED
D.L. MOODY

R A. Torrey
with a Biography & Sermons

RRMI
John 7:38

CHRISTIAN LIFE BOOKS
THE PUBLISHING ARM OF RIVER OF REVIVAL MINISTRIES, INC.
DUNCAN OK 73534

Why God Used D. L. Moody
Copyright © 1923

Christian Life Books Edition
Copyright © 2008, 2024

All rights reserved. No portion of this book may be used without the written permission of the publisher, with the exception of brief excerpts in magazine articles, reviews, etc.

ISBN 978-1-931393-43-0

CHRISTIAN LIFE BOOKS
P.O. BOX 5
DUNCAN, OK 73534
WWW.RRMI.ORG
WWW.AZUSASTREET.ORG
DRLARRYMARTIN.ORG
PENTECOSTALGOLD.COM

info@azusastreet.org

CONTENTS

List of Illustrations

FOREWORD

D. L. Moody has always been one of my heroes. Without doubt he was one of the greatest evangelists that ever lived—perhaps the very greatest. He personally preached to more than 100 million people. While others' lives have been tainted by scandal and greed, Moody, it seems, had an unblemished career.

In the spring of 2008, I had the privilege of visiting Northfield, Moody's home. I was awestruck as I saw the place of his birth, his death and much of his ministry. I stood in the pulpit where he preached, held his Bible, even wore his coat. I was most impressed by an article I saw in his mother's home. It was an abridged account of Torrey's *Why God Used D. L. Moody*. I was deeply touched. When I found the book was not readily available, I decided right away that Christian Life Books should put it into print so that a new generation could know the secrets to Moody's great power with God. I pray your life will be forever changed by it.

Larry Martin, D.Min., Editor

Moody's Signature

A Consecrated Life
D.L. Moody

Author Unknown

Moody in His Later Years

A CONSECRATED LIFE:

THE LATE EVANGELIST MOODY & HIS WORK FOR THE MASTER

"Some day you will be told that Moody is dead. Don't believe a word of it. At that very moment I shall be more truly alive than I am now. I shall then be beginning to live. I was born of the flesh on February 5, 1837. I was born of the Spirit in 1856. That which was born of the flesh will die, of course; but that which is born of the Spirit will live forever."

These were the words of America's greatest evangelist, spoken at a meeting in 1898. He passed away on December 29, 1899.

The man who was to address the largest audiences ever gathered for religious teaching, who was destined to win souls in numbers so enormous, came out of a little New England village, with no advantages of education and no ecclesiastical or academic training for his work. Almost within sight of the home at Northfield, in which he died, was the humble cottage in which he first saw the light. His father died suddenly, leaving nine children for his widow to support on a mortgaged farm. Mr. Moody often spoke in later years of the splendid courage his honored mother displayed in the emergency. It must have been a hard struggle, but her children stood by her loyally. "Dwight used to think himself a man when he was only a boy," his mother would say in after years.

When only six years old he went to a farmer and engaged himself as a hired help, his duty being to drive the cows to and from their pasture morning and evening. The sturdy independence of the lad was astonishing in one of his age, He worked on the farm, getting such educational help as the village school afforded until he was seventeen, when he felt that the time had come for him to enter a wider sphere. His mother had a brother in Boston engaged in the shoe business, and to him young Moody went to get employment. The wise man accepted his nephew's offer, but made three conditions. The boy must live in a boarding house of his uncle's selection; he must not wander about the city in the evening, nor go to places of amusement of which his uncle did not approve; and he must regularly attend the Mount Vernon church and Sunday school. The boy agreed to all and honorably kept his bargain. The third condition appears to have been a little irksome at first, but before two years had passed Dwight L. Moody was an applicant for membership in the church, and was admitted.

In the fall of 1856 Mr. Moody removed to Chicago, where he found employment as clerk in a shoe store. He united with the Plymouth Congregational Church and volunteered for Sunday school work. He does not appear to have met with much encouragement. He surprised the trustees by hiring four pews, which was an unusual thing for a bachelor to do. But it was his habit to look up any young men whom he could get acquainted with, and he would invite them to occupy his pews. They were filled at every service. He also found a little mission church in North Wells street which seemed to be in need of help, and he offered his services as a teacher in the Sunday school. He was told that there were already teachers for all the classes, but if he would bring new pupils he could form another class. The next Sunday he marched in at the head of eighteen barefooted children, whom he had collected out of the slums. Each one, he reminded the superintendent, had a soul to be saved, unpromising as the material looked. The class grew so rapidly and received additions of so many older members, that Mr. Moody rented an empty saloon for its accommodation.

In a short time he had a Sunday school of his own, with seven hundred children and sixty teachers. Larger quarters becoming necessary, Mr. Moody obtained the use of a large room over the old North Market, which was used on Saturday nights for dancing. After the dances were over, Mr. Moody took possession of the room and with his own hands swept and cleaned it and prepared it for the meeting of the Sunday school. He also opened it for a week evening service, to which, in some way known only to himself, he brought a motley audience. Like his Master he sought out the neglected and the lost, and found his hearers among the heathen of the city. So fascinated did he become in this work, that he took the bold step of giving up his business to devote all his time to it, "But how are you going to live?" asked a practical friend, to whom he announced the step he had taken. "I don't know," Mr. Moody replied, "but I can stand it for several weeks, and if at the end of that time God wishes me to keep on, he will provide the means. He can, you know." Mr. Moody's faith was justified by results. In a short time the work outgrew its quarters, and Mr. John V. Farwell came to its relief by erecting Farwell Hall, which had accommodations for the Y.M.C.A. as well as for Mr. Moody's mission.

The outbreak of the Civil War turned Mr. Moody's attention temporarily in another direction. He visited the camps and made addresses to the soldiers. There he first realized his power as a speaker and acquired that manly, argumentative style of talk which characterized all his subsequent addresses. After the war he resumed his evangelizing of the slums of Chicago. Farwell Hall was burned, but Mr. Moody refused to regard the destruction as an intimation that his work there was ended. While the ruins were still smoking, he was around among the business men of the city with a subscription paper, and as soon as it was possible to occupy the ground, he had the funds in hand for the erection of a new building, and the plans for it in the builders' hands.

The mission grew with such rapidity that in 1863 it was necessary to erect a church building. Mr. Moody married, and a career of increasing usefulness and prosperity as a city pastor appeared to be opening before him. The great fire, however, changed that prospect. Mr. Moody was called to serve in the great cities, and to minister to the church universal. The great meetings in the Hippodrome, New York, convinced him (if he had needed conviction) of the character of his future work.

It is unnecessary to tell here the story of his campaigns, in which, accompanied by Mr. Ira D. Sankey, he went to every city from the Atlantic to the Pacific, and from Canada to the Gulf. On the other side the Atlantic the triumphs were as great. No buildings were large enough to hold the people who thronged to hear a plain man, in strong, forcible Anglo-Saxon words, explain the way of salvation. Wherever he spoke, either in his own land or across the Atlantic, the common people heard him gladly; and men like Drummond and Gladstone, highly educated as they were, sat at his feet delighted.

Exhausting as such labors were, Mr. Moody's energies were not satisfied. The enterprises at Northfield testify to his boundless activity. The Seminary for Girls, established in 1879, was the beginning of an educational work which has developed with phenomenal rapidity. The Chicago Institute, the School for Boys at Mount Hermon, and the numerous buildings at Northfield— which make, up a town of themselves are all memorials of the devotion and consecration with which he applied himself to the Master's service. Nor did these alone exhaust his energy. In later years his summer schools— in which many a minister gained new inspiration for his work—won for him the gratitude of the churches. Besides these, his pen was always busy, and his Colportage Library penetrated with its Gospel literature to every corner of the English-speaking world. To the last moment of his life he was devising new methods of service, and was looking forward to labors still more abundant.

In the course of a noble eulogy at the funeral service, Bishop Mallalieu paid this glowing tribute to the great Evangelist:

"The heart of no disciple of the Master ever beat with more genuine, sympathetic, and utterly unselfish loyalty than did this great heart. Because he held fast to the absolute truth of the Bible, and unequivocally and intensely believed it to be the inerrant Word of God; because he preached the Gospel rather than talked about the Gospel; because he used his mother tongue, the terse, clear, ringing, straight-forward Saxon; because he had the profoundest sense of brotherhood with all poor, unfortunate, and even outcast people; because he was unaffectedly tender and patient with the weak and sinful; because he hated evil as thoroughly as he loved goodness; because he knew right how to lead penitent souls to the Savior; because he had the rare and happy art of arousing Christian people to the performance of their duties; because he had in his own soul a conscious, joyous experience of personal salvation, the people flocked to his services, they heard him gladly, they were led to Christ, and he came to be prized and honored by all denominations, so that Protestantism recognizes the fact that he was God's servant, an ambassador of Christ, and, indeed, a chosen vessel to bear the name of Jesus to the nations."

From *Thou Fool and Eleven Other Sermons*, 1911.

WHY GOD USED
D.L. MOODY

BY R. A. TORREY

D. L. Moody and Ira D. Sankey

WHY GOD USED D. L. MOODY

Eighty-six years ago (February 5, 1837), there was born of poor parents in a humble farmhouse in Northfield, Massachusetts, a little baby who was to become the greatest man, as I believe, of his generation or of his century—Dwight L. Moody. After our great generals, great statesmen, great scientists and great men of letters have passed away and been forgotten, and their work and its helpful influence has come to an end, the work of D. L. Moody will go on and its saving influence continue and increase, bringing blessing not only to every state in the Union but to every nation on earth. Yes, it will continue throughout the ages of eternity.

My subject is "Why God Used D. L. Moody," and I can think of no subject upon which I would rather speak. For I shall not seek to glorify Mr. Moody, but the God who by His grace, His entirely unmerited favor, used him so mightily, and the Christ who saved him by His atoning death and resurrection life, and the Holy Spirit who lived in him and wrought through him and who alone made him the mighty power that he was to this world. Furthermore, I hope to make it clear that the God who used D. L. Moody in his day is just as ready to use you and me, in this day, if we, on our part, do what D. L. Moody did, which was what made it possible for God to so abundantly use him.

The whole secret of why D. L. Moody was such a mightily used man you will find in Psalm 62:11: "God hath spoken once; twice have I heard this; that *power belongeth unto God.*" I am glad it does. I am glad that power did not belong to D. L. Moody; I am glad that it did not belong to Charles G. Finney; I am glad that it did not belong to Martin Luther; I am glad that it did not belong to any other Christian man whom God has greatly used in this world's history. Power belongs to God. If D. L. Moody had any power, and he had great power, he got it from God.

But God does not give His power arbitrarily. It is true that He gives it to whomsoever He will, but He wills to give it on certain conditions, which are clearly revealed in His Word; and D. L. Moody met those conditions and God made him the most wonderful preacher of his generation; yes, I think the most wonderful man of his generation.

But how was it that D. L. Moody had that power of God so wonderfully manifested in his life? Pondering this question it seemed to me that there were seven things in the life of D. L. Moody that accounted for God's using him so largely as He did.

1

A FULLY SURRENDERED MAN

The first thing that accounts for God's using D. L. Moody so mightily was that he was a fully surrendered man. Every ounce of that two-hundred-and-eighty-pound body of his belonged to God; everything he was and everything he had, belonged wholly to God. Now, I am not saying that Mr. Moody was perfect; he was not. If I attempted to, I presume I could point out some defects in his character. It does not occur to me at this moment what they were; but I am confident that I could think of some, if I tried real hard. I have never yet met a perfect man, not one. I have known perfect men in the sense in which the Bible commands us to be perfect, i.e., men who are wholly God's, out and out for God, fully surrendered to God, with no will but God's will; but I have never known a man in whom I could not see some defects, some places where he might have been improved.

No, Mr. Moody was not a faultless man. If he had any flaws in his character, and he had, I presume I was in a position to know them better than almost any other man, because of my very close association with him in the later years of his life; and furthermore, I suppose that in his latter days he opened his heart to me more fully than to anyone else in the world. I think He told me some things that he told no one else. I presume I knew whatever defects there were in his character as well as anybody. But while I recognized such flaws, nevertheless, I know that he was a man who belonged wholly to God.

The first month I was in Chicago, we were having a talk about something upon which we very widely differed, and Mr. Moody turned to me very frankly and very kindly and said in defense of his own position: "Torrey, if I believed that God wanted me to jump out of that window, I would jump." I believe he would. If he thought God wanted him to do anything, he would do it. He belonged wholly, unreservedly, unqualifiedly, entirely, to God.

Henry Varley, a very intimate friend of Mr. Moody in the earlier days of his work, loved to tell how he once said to him: "It remains to be seen what God will do with a man who gives himself up wholly to Him." I am told that when Mr. Henry Varley said that, Mr. Moody said to himself: "Well, I will be that man." And I, for my part, do not think "it remains to be seen" what God will do with a man who gives himself up wholly to Him. I think it has been seen already in D. L. Moody.

If you and I are to be used in our sphere as D. L. Moody was used in his, we must put all that we have and all that we are in the hands of God, for Him to use as He will, to send us where He will, for God to do with us what He will, and we, on our part, to do everything God bids us do.

There are thousands and tens of thousands of men and women in Christian work, brilliant men and women, rarely gifted men and women, men and women who are making great sacrifices, men and women who have put all conscious sin out of their lives, yet who, nevertheless, have stopped short of absolute surrender to God, and therefore have stopped short of fullness of power. But Mr. Moody did not stop short of absolute surrender to God; he was a wholly surrendered man, and if you and I are to be used, you and I must be wholly surrendered men and women.

A Sketch of Moody Preaching

2
A MAN OF PRAYER

The second secret of the great power exhibited in Mr. Moody's life was that Mr. Moody was in the deepest and most meaningful sense a man of prayer. People oftentimes say to me: "Well, I went many miles to see and to hear D. L. Moody and he certainly was a wonderful preacher." Yes, D. L. Moody certainly was a wonderful preacher; taking it all in all, the most wonderful preacher I have ever heard, and it was a great privilege to hear him preach as he alone could preach; but out of a very intimate acquaintance with him I wish to testify that he was a far greater pray-er than he was preacher.

Time and time again, he was confronted by obstacles that seemed insurmountable, but he always knew the way to surmount and to overcome all difficulties. He knew the way to bring to pass anything that needed to be brought to pass. He knew and believed in the deepest depths of his soul that "nothing was too hard for the Lord" and that prayer could do anything that God could do.

Often times Mr. Moody would write me when he was about to undertake some new work, saying: "I am beginning work in such and such a place on such and such a day; I wish you would get the students together for a day of fasting and prayer" And often I have taken those letters and read them to the students in the lecture room and said: "Mr. Moody wants us to have a day of fasting and prayer, first for God's blessing on our own souls and work, and then for God's blessing on him and his work."

Often we were gathered in the lecture room far into the night—sometimes till one, two, three, four or even five o'clock in the morning, crying to God, just because Mr. Moody urged us to wait upon God until we received His blessing. How many men and women I have known whose lives and characters have been transformed by those nights of prayer and who have wrought mighty things in many lands because of those nights of prayer!

One day Mr. Moody drove up to my house at Northfield and said: "Torrey, I want you to take a ride with me." I got into the carriage and we drove out toward Lover's Lane, talking about some great and unexpected difficulties that had arisen in regard to the work in Northfield and Chicago, and in connection with other work that was very dear to him.

As we drove along, some black storm clouds lay ahead of us, and then suddenly, as we were talking, it began to rain. He drove the horse into a shed near the entrance to Lover's Lane to shelter the horse, and then laid the reins upon the dashboard and said: "Torrey, pray;" and then, as best I could, I prayed, while he in his heart joined me in prayer. And when my voice was silent he began to pray. Oh, I wish you could have heard that prayer! I shall never forget it, so simple, so trustful, so definite and so direct and so mighty. When the storm was over and we drove back to town, the obstacles had been surmounted, and the work of the schools, and other work that was threatened, went on as it had never gone on before, and it has gone on until this day.

As we drove back, Mr. Moody said to me: "Torrey, we will let the other men do the talking and the criticizing, and we will stick to the work that God has given us to do, and let Him take care of the difficulties and answer the criticisms."

On one occasion Mr. Moody said to me in Chicago: "I have just found, to my surprise, that we are twenty thousand dollars behind in our finances for the work here and in Northfield, and we must have that twenty thousand dollars, and I am going to get it by prayer." He did not tell a soul who had the ability to give a penny of the twenty thousand dollars deficit, but looked right to God and said: "I need twenty thousand dollars for my work; send me that money in such a way that I will know it comes straight from Thee." And God heard that prayer. The money came in such a way that it was clear that it came from God in direct answer to prayer.

Yes, D. L. Moody was a man who believed in the God who answers prayer, and not only believed in Him in a theoretical way but believed in Him in a practical way. He was a man who met every difficulty that stood in his way—by prayer. Everything he undertook was backed up by prayer, and in everything, his ultimate dependence was upon God.

Moody and His Sunday School Boys.

3

A DEEP AND PRACTICAL
STUDENT OF THE BIBLE

The third secret of Mr. Moody's power, or the third reason why God used D. L. Moody, was because he was a deep and practical student of the Word of God. Nowadays it is often said of D. L. Moody that he was not a student. I wish to say that he was a student; most emphatically he was a student. He was not a student of psychology; he was not a student of anthropology—I am very sure he would not have known what that word meant; he was not a student of biology; he was not a student of philosophy; he was not even a student of theology, in the technical sense of the term; but he was a student, a profound and practical student of the one Book that is more worth studying than all other books in the world put together; he was a student of the Bible.

Every day of his life, I have reason for believing, he arose very early in the morning to study the Bible. He would say to me: "If I am going to get in any study, I have got to get up before the other folks get up;" and he would shut himself up in a remote room in his house, alone with his God and his Bible.

I shall never forget the first night I spent in his home. He had invited me to take the superintendency of the Bible Institute and I had already begun my work; I was on my way to some city in the East to preside at the International Christian Workers' Convention. He wrote me saying: "Just as soon as the Convention is over, come up to Northfield." He learned when I was likely to arrive and drove over to South Vernon to meet me. That night he had all the teachers from the Mount Hermon School and from the Northfield Seminary come together at the house to meet me, and to talk over the problems of the two schools. We talked together far on into the night, and then, after the principals and teachers of the schools had gone home, Mr. Moody and I talked together about the problems a while longer.

It was very late when I got to bed that night, but very early the next morning, about five o'clock, I heard a gentle tap on my door. Then I heard Mr. Moody's voice whispering: "Torrey, are you up?" I happened to be; I do not always get up at that early hour but I happened to be up that particular morning. He said: "I want you to go somewhere with me," and I went down with him. Then I found out that he had already been up an hour or two in his room studying the Word of God.

Oh, you may talk about power; but, if you neglect the one Book that God has given you as the one instrument through which He imparts and exercises His power, you will not have it. You may read many books and go to many conventions and you may have your all-night prayer meetings to pray for the power of the Holy Ghost; but unless you keep in constant and close association with the one Book, the Bible, you will not have power. And if you ever had power, you will not maintain it except by the daily, earnest, intense study of that Book.

Ninety-nine Christians in every hundred are merely playing at Bible study; and therefore ninety-nine Christians in every hundred are mere weaklings, when they might be giants, both in their Christian life and in their service.

It was largely because of his thorough knowledge of the Bible, and his practical knowledge of the Bible, that Mr. Moody drew such immense crowds. On "Chicago Day," in October, 1893, none of the theaters of Chicago dared to open because it was expected that everybody in Chicago would go on that day to the World's Fair; and, in point of fact, something like four hundred thousand people did pass through the gates of the Fair that day. Everybody in Chicago was expected to be at that end of the city on that day. But Mr. Moody said to me: "Torrey, engage the Central Music Hall and announce meetings from nine o'clock in the morning till six o'clock at night." "Why," I replied, "Mr. Moody, nobody will be at this end of Chicago on that day; not even the theaters dare to open; everybody is going down to Jackson Park to the Fair; we cannot get anybody out on this day."

Mr. Moody replied: "You do as you are told;" and I did as I was told and engaged the Central Music Hall for continuous meetings from nine o'clock in the morning till six o'clock at night. But I did it with a heavy heart; I thought there would be poor audiences. I was on the program at noon that day Being very busy in my office about the details of the campaign, I did not reach the Central Music Hall till almost noon. I thought I would have no trouble in getting in. But when I got almost to the Hall I found to my amazement that not only was it packed but the vestibule was packed and the steps were packed, and there was no getting anywhere near the door; and if I had not gone round and climbed in a back window they would have lost their speaker for that hour. But that would not have been of much importance, for the crowds had not gathered to hear me; it was the magic of Mr. Moody's name that had drawn them. And why did they long to hear Mr. Moody? Because they knew that while he was not versed in many of the philosophies and fads and fancies of the day, he did know the one Book that this old world most longs to know—the Bible.

I shall never forget Moody's last visit to Chicago. The ministers of Chicago had sent me to Cincinnati to invite him to come to Chicago and hold a meeting. In response to the invitation, Mr. Moody said to me: "If you will hire the Auditorium for weekday mornings and afternoons and have meetings at ten in the morning and three in the afternoon, I will go." I replied: "Mr. Moody, you know what a busy city Chicago is, and how impossible it is for businessmen to get out at ten o'clock in the morning and three in the afternoon on working days. Will you not hold evening meetings and meetings on Sunday?" "No," he replied, "I am afraid if I did, I would interfere with the regular work of the churches."

I went back to Chicago and engaged the Auditorium, which at that time was the building having the largest seating capacity of any building in the city, seating in those days about seven thousand people; I announced weekday meetings, with Mr. Moody as the speaker, at ten o'clock in the mornings and three o'clock in the afternoons.

At once protests began to pour in upon me. One of them came from Marshall Field, at that time the business king of Chicago. "Mr. Torrey," Mr. Field wrote, "we businessmen of Chicago wish to hear Mr. Moody, and you know perfectly well how impossible it is for us to get out at ten o'clock in the morning and three o'clock in the afternoon; have evening meetings." I received many letters of a similar purport and wrote to Mr. Moody urging him to give us evening meetings. But Mr. Moody simply replied: "You do as you are told," and I did as I was told; that is the way I kept my job.

On the first morning of the meetings I went down to the Auditorium about half an hour before the appointed time, but I went with much fear and apprehension; I thought the Auditorium would be nowhere nearly full. When I reached there, to my amazement I found a queue of people four abreast extending from the Congress Street entrance to Wabash Avenue, then a block north on Wabash Avenue, then a break to let traffic through, and then another block, and so on. I went in through the back door, and there were many clamoring for entrance there. When the doors were opened at the appointed time, we had a cordon of twenty policemen to keep back the crowd; but the crowd was so great that it swept the cordon of policemen off their feet and packed eight thousand people into the building before we could get the doors shut. And I think there were as many left on the outside as there were in the building. I do not think that anyone else in the world could have drawn such a crowd at such a time.

Why? Because though Mr. Moody knew little about science or philosophy or literature in general, he did know the one Book that this old world is perishing to know and longing to know; and this old world will flock to hear men who know the Bible and preach the Bible as they will flock to hear nothing else on earth.

During all the months of the World's Fair in Chicago, no one could draw such crowds as Mr. Moody. Judging by the papers, one would have thought that the great religious event in Chicago at that time was the World's Congress of Religions. One very gifted man of letters in the East was invited to speak at this Congress. He saw in this invitation the opportunity of his life and prepared his paper, the exact title of which I do not now recall, but it was something along the line of "New Light on the Old Doctrines." He prepared the paper with great care, and then sent it around to his most trusted and gifted friends for criticisms. These men sent it back to him with such emendations as they had to suggest. Then he rewrote the paper, incorporating as many of the suggestions and criticisms as seemed wise. Then he sent it around for further criticisms. Then he wrote the paper a third time, and had it, as he trusted, perfect. He went on to Chicago to meet this coveted opportunity of speaking at the World's Congress of Religions.

It was at eleven o'clock on a Saturday morning (if I remember correctly) that he was to speak. He stood outside the door of the platform waiting for the great moment to arrive, and as the clock struck eleven he walked on to the platform to face a magnificent audience of eleven women and two men! But there was not a building anywhere in Chicago that would accommodate the very same day the crowds that would flock to hear Mr. Moody at any hour of the day or night.

Oh, men and women, if you wish to get an audience and wish to do that audience some good after you get them, study, study, *study* the one Book, and preach, preach, *preach* the one Book, and teach, teach, *teach* the one Book, the Bible, the only Book that is God's Word, and the only Book that has power to gather and hold and bless the crowds for any great length of time.

Moody Preaching to a Massive Crowd

4
A HUMBLE MAN UNTO GOD

The fourth reason why God continuously through so many years, used D.L. Moody was because he was a humble man. I think D. L. Moody was the humblest man I ever knew in all my life. He loved to quote the words of another; "Faith gets the most; love works the most; but humility keeps the most."

He himself had the humility that keeps everything it gets. As I have already said, he was the most humble man I ever knew, i.e., the most humble man when we bear in mind the great things that he did, and the praise that was lavished upon him. Oh, how he loved to put himself in the background and put other men in the foreground. How often he would stand on a platform with some of us little fellows seated behind him and as he spoke he would say: "There are better men coming after me." As he said it, he would point back over his shoulder with his thumb to the "little fellows. " I do not know how he could believe it, but he really did believe that the others that were coming after him were really better than he was. He made no pretense to a humility he did not possess. In his heart of hearts he constantly underestimated himself, and overestimated others.

He really believed that God would use other men in a larger measure than he had been used. Mr. Moody loved to keep himself in the background. At his conventions at Northfield, or anywhere else, he would push the other men to the front and, if he could, have them do all the preaching—McGregor, Campbell Morgan, Andrew Murray, and the rest of them. The only way we could get him to take any part in the program was to get up in the convention and move that we hear D. L. Moody at the next meeting. He continually put himself out of sight.

Oh, how many a man has been full of promise and God has used him, and then the man thought that he was the whole thing and God was compelled to set him aside! I believe more promising workers have gone on the rocks through self-sufficiency and self-esteem than through any other cause. I can look back for forty years, or more, and think of many men who are now wrecks or derelicts who at one time the world thought were going to be something great. But they have disappeared entirely from the public view. Why? Because of over-estimation of self. Oh, the men and women who have been put aside because they began to think that they were somebody, that they were "*it*," and therefore God was compelled to set them aside.

I remember a man with whom I was closely associated in a great movement in this country. We were having a most successful convention in Buffalo, and he was greatly elated. As we walked down the street together to one of the meetings one day he said to me: "Torrey, you and

I are the most important men in Christian work in this country." or words to that effect. I replied: "John, I am sorry to hear you say that; for as I read my Bible I find man after man who had accomplished great things whom God had to set aside because of his sense of his own importance." And God set that man aside also from that time. I think he is still living, but no one ever hears of him, or has heard of him for years.

God used D. L. Moody, I think, beyond any man of his day; but it made no difference how much God used him, he never was puffed up. One day, speaking to me of a great New York preacher, now dead, Mr. Moody said: "He once did a very foolish thing, the most foolish thing that I ever knew a man, ordinarily so wise as he was, to do. He came up to me at the close of a little talk I had given and said: 'Young man, you have made a great address tonight.'" Then Mr. Moody continued: "How foolish of him to have said that! It almost turned my head." But, thank God, it did not turn his head, and even when pretty much all the ministers in England, Scotland and Ireland, and many of the English bishops were ready to follow D. L. Moody wherever he led, even then it never turned his head one bit. He would get down on his face before God, knowing he was human, and ask God to empty him of all self-sufficiency. And God did.

Oh, men and women! especially young men and young women, perhaps God is beginning to use you; very likely people are saying: "What a wonderful gift he has as a Bible teacher, what power he has as a preacher, for such a young man!" Listen: get down upon your face before God. I believe here lies one of the most dangerous snares of the Devil. When the Devil cannot discourage a man, he approaches him on another tack, which he knows is far worse in its results; he puffs him up by whispering in his ear: "You are the leading evangelist of the day. You are the man who will sweep everything before you. You are the coming man. You are the D. L. Moody of the day;" and if you listen to him, he will ruin you. The entire shore of the history of Christian workers is strewn with the wrecks of gallant vessels that were full of promise a few years ago, but these men became puffed up and were driven on the rocks by the wild winds of their own raging self-esteem.

5

HIS ENTIRE FREEDOM
FROM THE LOVE OF MONEY

The fifth secret of D. L. Moody's continual power and usefulness was his entire freedom from the love of money. Mr. Moody might have been a wealthy man, but money had no charms for him. He loved to gather money for God's work; he refused to accumulate money for himself. He told me during the World's Fair that if he had taken, for himself, the royalties on the hymnbooks which he had published, they would have amounted, at that time, to a million dollars. But Mr. Moody refused to touch the money. He had a perfect right to take it, for he was responsible for the publication of the books and it was his money that went into the publication of the first of them.

Mr. Sankey had some hymns that he had taken with him to England and he wished to have them published. He went to a publisher (I think Morgan & Scott) and they declined to publish them, because, as they said, Philip Phillips had recently been over and published a hymnbook and it had not done well. However, Mr. Moody had a little money and he said that he would put it into the publication of these hymns in cheap form; and he did. The hymns had a most remarkable and unexpected sale; they were then published in book form and large profits accrued. The financial results were offered to Mr. Moody, but he refused to touch them. "But," it was urged on him, "the money belongs to you;" but he would not touch it.

Mr. Fleming H. Revell was at the time treasurer of the Chicago Avenue Church, commonly known as the Moody Tabernacle. Only the basement of this new church building had been completed, funds having been exhausted. Hearing of the hymnbook situation Mr. Revell suggested, in a letter to friends in London, that the money be given for completion of this building, and it was. Afterwards, so much money came in that it was given, by the committee into whose hands Mr. Moody put the matter, to various Christian enterprises.

In a certain city to which Mr. Moody went in the latter years of his life, and where I went with him, it was publicly announced that Mr. Moody would accept no money whatever for his services. Now, in point of fact, Mr. Moody was dependent, in a measure, upon what was given him at various services; but when this announcement was made, Mr. Moody said nothing, and left that city without a penny's compensation for the hard work he did there; and, I think, he paid his own hotel bill. And yet a minister in that very city came out with an article in a paper, which I read, in which he told a fairy tale of the financial demands that Mr. Moody made upon them, which story I knew personally to be absolutely untrue. Millions of dollars passed into Mr.

Moody hands, but they passed through; they did not stick to his fingers.

This is the point at which many an evangelist makes shipwreck, and his great work comes to an untimely end. The love of money on the part of some evangelists has done more to discredit evangelistic work in our day, and to lay many an evangelist on the shelf, than almost any other cause.

While I was away on my recent tour I was told by one of the most reliable ministers in one of our eastern cities of a campaign conducted by one who has been greatly used in the past. (Do not imagine, for a moment, that I am speaking of Billy Sunday, for I am not; this same minister spoke in the highest terms of Mr. Sunday and of a campaign which he conducted in a city where this minister was a pastor.) This evangelist of whom I now speak came to a city for a united evangelistic campaign and was supported by fifty-three churches. The minister who told me about the matter was himself chairman of the Finance Committee.

The evangelist showed such a longing for money and so deliberately violated the agreement he had made before coming to the city and so insisted upon money being gathered for him in other ways than he had himself prescribed in the original contract, that this minister threatened to resign from the Finance Committee. He was, however, persuaded to remain to avoid a scandal. "As the total result of the three weeks campaign there were only twenty-four clear decisions," said my friend; "and after it was over the ministers got together and by a vote with but one dissenting voice, they agreed to send a letter to this evangelist telling him frankly that they were done with him and with his methods of evangelism forever, and that they felt it their duty to warn other cities against him and his methods and the results of his work." Let us lay the lesson to our hearts and take warning in time.

6

HIS CONSUMING PASSION FOR THE SALVATION OF THE LOST

The sixth reason why God used D. L. Moody was because of his consuming passion for the salvation of the lost. Mr. Moody made the resolution, shortly after he himself was saved, that he would never let twenty-four hours pass over his head without speaking to at least one person about his soul. His was a very busy life, and sometimes he would forget his resolution until the last hour, and sometimes he would get out of bed, dress, go out and talk to someone about his soul in order that he might not let one day pass without having definitely told at least one of his fellow-mortals about his need and the Savior who could meet it.

One night Mr. Moody was going home from his place of business. It was very late, and it suddenly occurred to him that he had not spoken to one single person that day about accepting Christ. He said to himself: "Here's a day lost. I have not spoken to anyone today and I shall not see anybody at this late hour." But as he walked up the street he saw a man standing under a lamppost. The man was a perfect stranger to him, though it turned out afterwards the man knew who Mr. Moody was. He stepped up to this stranger and said: "Are you a Christian?" The man replied: "That is none of your business, whether I am a Christian or not. If you were not a sort of a preacher I would knock you into the gutter for your impertinence." Mr. Moody said a few earnest words and passed on.

The next day that man called upon one of Mr. Moody's prominent business friends and said to him: "That man Moody of yours over on the North Side is doing more harm than he is good. He has got zeal without knowledge. He stepped up to me last night, a perfect stranger, and insulted me. He asked me if I were a Christian, and I told him it was none of his business and if he were not a sort of a preacher I would knock him into the gutter for his impertinence. He is doing more harm than he is good. He has got zeal without knowledge." Mr. Moody's friend sent for him and said: "Moody, you are doing more harm than you are good; you've got zeal without knowledge: you insulted a friend of mine on the street last night. You went up to him, a perfect stranger, and asked him if he were a Christian, and he tells me if you had not been a sort of a preacher he would have knocked you into the gutter for your impertinence. You are doing more harm than you are good; you have got zeal without knowledge."

Mr. Moody went out of that man's office somewhat crestfallen. He wondered if he were not doing more harm than he was good, if he really had zeal without knowledge. (Let me say, in passing, it is far better to have zeal without knowledge than it is to have knowledge without zeal. Some men and women are as full of knowledge as an egg is of meat; they are so deeply versed in Bible truth that they can sit in criticism on the preachers and give the preachers pointers, but they have so little zeal that they do not lead one soul to Christ in a whole year.)

Weeks passed by. One night Mr. Moody was in bed when he heard a tremendous pounding at his front door. He jumped out of bed and rushed to the door. He thought the house was on fire. He thought the man would break down the door. He opened the door and there stood this man. He said: "Mr. Moody, I have not had a good night's sleep since that night you spoke to me under the lamppost, and I have come around at this unearthly hour of the night for you to tell me what I have to do to be saved." Mr. Moody took him in and told him what to do to be saved. Then he accepted Christ, and when the Civil War broke out, he went to the front and laid down his life fighting for his country.

Another night, Mr. Moody got home and had gone to bed before it occurred to him that he had not spoken to a soul that day about accepting Christ. "Well," he said to himself, "it is no good getting up now; there will be nobody on the street at this hour of the night." But he got up, dressed and went to the front door. It was pouring rain. "Oh," he said, "there will be no one out in this pouring rain. Just then he heard the patter of a man's feet as he came down the street, holding an umbrella over his head. Then Mr. Moody darted out and rushed up to the man and said: "May I share the shelter of your umbrella?" "Certainly," the man replied. Then Mr. Moody said: "Have you any shelter in the time of storm?" and preached Jesus to him. Oh, men and women, if we were as full of zeal for the salvation of souls as that, how long would it be before the whole country would be shaken by the power of a mighty, God-sent revival?

One day in Chicago—the day after the elder Carter Harrison was shot, when his body was lying in state in the City Hall—Mr. Moody and I were riding up Randolph Street together in a streetcar right alongside of the City Hall. The car could scarcely get through because of the enormous crowds waiting to get in and view the body of Mayor Harrison. As the car tried to push its way through the crowd, Mr. Moody turned to me and said: "Torrey, what does this mean?" "Why," I said, "Carter Harrison's body lies there in the City Hall and these crowds are waiting to see it."

Then he said: "This will never do, to let these crowds get away from us without preaching to them; we must talk to them. You go and hire Hooley's Opera House (which was just opposite the City Hall) for the whole day." I did so. The meetings began at nine o'clock in the morning, and we had one continuous service from that hour until six in the evening, to reach those crowds.

Mr. Moody was a man on fire for God. Not only was he always "on the job" himself but he was always getting others to work as well. He once invited me down to Northfield to spend a month there with the schools, speaking first to one school and then crossing the river to the other. I was obliged to use the ferry a great deal; it was before the present bridge was built at that point.

One day he said to me: "Torrey did you know that that ferryman that ferries you across every day was unconverted?" He did not tell me to speak to him, but I knew what he meant. When some days later it was told him that the ferryman was saved, he was exceedingly happy.

Once, when walking down a certain street in Chicago, Mr. Moody stepped up to a man, a perfect stranger to him, and said: "Sir, are you a Christian?" "You mind your own business," was the reply. Mr. Moody replied: "This is my business." The man said, "Well, then, you must be Moody." Out in Chicago they used to call him in those early days "Crazy Moody," because day and night he was speaking to everybody he got a chance to speak to about being saved.

One time he was going to Milwaukee, and in the seat that he had chosen sat a traveling man. Mr. Moody sat down beside him and immediately began to talk with him. "Where are you going?" Mr. Moody asked. When told the name of the town he said: "We will soon be there; we'll have to get down to business at once. Are you saved?" The man said that he was not, and Mr. Moody took out his Bible and there on the train showed him the way of salvation. Then he said: "Now, you must take Christ." The man did; he was converted right there on the train.

Most of you have heard, I presume, the story President Wilson used to tell about D. L. Moody. Ex-President Wilson said that he once went into a barber shop and took a chair next to the one in which D. L. Moody was sitting, though he did not know that Mr. Moody was there. He had not been in the chair very long before, as ex-President Wilson phrased it, he "knew there was a personality in the other chair," and he began to listen to the conversation going on; he heard Mr. Moody tell the barber about the Way of Life, and President Wilson said, "I have never forgotten that scene to this day." When Mr. Moody was gone, he asked the barber who he was; when he was told that it was D. L. Moody, President Wilson said: "It made an impression upon me I have not yet forgotten."

On one occasion in Chicago Mr. Moody saw a little girl standing on the street with a pail in her hand. He went up to her and invited her to his Sunday school, telling her what a pleasant place it was. She promised to go the following Sunday, but she did not do so. Mr. Moody watched for her for weeks, and then one day he saw her on the street again, at some distance from him. He started toward her, but she saw him too and started to run away. Mr. Moody followed her. Down she went one street, Mr. Moody after her; up she went another street, Mr. Moody after her, through an alley, Mr. Moody still following; out on another street, Mr. Moody after her; then she dashed into a saloon and Mr. Moody dashed after her. She ran out the back door and up a flight of stairs, Mr. Moody still following; she dashed into a room, Mr. Moody following; she threw herself under the bed and Mr. Moody reached under the bed and pulled her out by the foot, and led her to Christ.

He found that her mother was a widow who had once seen better circumstances, but had gone down until now she was living over this saloon. She had several children. Mr. Moody led the mother and all the family to Christ. Several of the children were prominent members of the Moody Church until they moved away, and afterwards became prominent in churches elsewhere. This particular child, whom he pulled from underneath the bed, was, when I was the pastor of the Moody Church, the wife of one of the most prominent officers in the church.

Only two or three years ago, as I came out of a ticket office in Memphis, Tennessee, a fine-looking young man followed me. He said: "Are you not Dr. Torrey?" I said, "Yes." He said: "I am so and so." He was the son of this woman. He was then a traveling man, and an officer in the church where he lived. When Mr. Moody pulled that little child out from under the bed by the foot he was pulling a whole family into the Kingdom of God, and eternity alone will reveal how many succeeding generations he was pulling into the Kingdom of God.

D. L. Moody's consuming passion for souls was not for the souls of those who would be helpful to him in building up his work here or elsewhere; his love for souls knew no class limitations. He was no respecter of persons; it might be an earl or a duke or it might be an ignorant colored boy* on the street; it was all the same to him; there was a soul to save and he did what lay in his power to save that soul.

A friend once told me that the first time he ever heard of Mr. Moody was when Mr. Reynolds of Peoria told him that he once found Mr. Moody sitting in one of the squatters' shanties that used to be in that part of the city toward the lake, which was then called, "The Sands," with a colored boy* on his knee, a tallow candle in one hand and a Bible in the other, and Mr. Moody was spelling out the words (for at that time the boy could not read very well) of certain verses of

---

*This language may seem inappropriate, or perhaps even racist to some today, but at the time of this writing it was considered respectful. No offense was or is intended. Ed.

Scripture, in an attempt to lead that ignorant colored boy* to Christ.

Oh, young men and women and all Christian workers, if you and I were on fire for souls like that, how long would it be before we had a revival? Suppose that tonight the fire of God falls and fills our hearts, a burning fire that will send us out all over the country and across the water to China, Japan, India and Africa, to tell lost souls the way of salvation!

7

DEFINITELY ENDUED WITH POWER FROM ON HIGH

The seventh thing that was the secret of why God used D. L. Moody was that he had a very definite enduement with power from on High, a very clear and definite baptism with the Holy Ghost. Moody knew he had "the baptism with the Holy Ghost;" he had no doubt about it. In his early days he was a great hustler; he had a tremendous desire to do something, but he had no real power. He worked very largely in the energy of the flesh.

But there were two humble Free Methodist women who used to come over to his meetings in the Y.M.C.A. One was "Auntie Cook" and the other, Mrs. Snow. (I think her name was not Snow at that time.) These two women would come to Mr. Moody at the close of his meetings and say: "We are praying for you." Finally Mr. Moody became somewhat nettled and said to them one night: "Why are you praying for me? Why don't you pray for the unsaved?" They replied: "We are praying that you may get the power." Mr. Moody did not know what that meant, but he got to thinking about it, and then went to these women and said: "I wish you would tell me what you mean;" and they told him about the definite baptism with the Holy Ghost. Then he asked that he might pray with them and not they merely pray for him.

Auntie Cook once told me of the intense fervor with which Mr. Moody prayed on that occasion. She told me in words that I scarcely dare repeat, though I have never forgotten them. And he not only prayed with them, but he also prayed alone.

Not long after, one day on his way to England, he was walking up Wall Street in New York; (Mr. Moody very seldom told this and I almost hesitate to tell it) and in the midst of the bustle and hurry of that city his prayer was answered; the power of God fell upon him as he walked up the street and he had to hurry off to the house of a friend and ask that he might have a room by himself, and in that room he stayed alone for hours; and the Holy Ghost came upon him, filling his soul with such joy that at last he had to ask God to withhold His hand, lest he die on the spot from very joy. He went out from that place with the power of the Holy Ghost upon him, and when he got to London (partly through the prayers of a bedridden saint in Mr. Lessey's church), the power of God wrought through him mightily in North London, and hundreds were added to the churches; and that was what led to his being invited over to the wonderful campaign that followed in later years.

Time and again Mr. Moody would come to me and say: "Torrey, I want you to preach on the baptism with the Holy Ghost." I do not know how many times he asked me to speak on that subject. Once, when I had been invited to preach in the Fifth Avenue Presbyterian Church, New York (invited at Mr. Moody's suggestion; had it not been for his suggestion the invitation would never have been extended to me), just before I started for New York, Mr. Moody drove up to my house and said: "Torrey, they want you to preach at the Fifth Avenue Presbyterian Church in New York. It is a great big church, cost a million dollars to build it." Then he continued: "Torrey, I just want to ask one thing of you. I want to tell you what to preach about. You will preach that sermon of yours on 'Ten Reasons Why I Believe the Bible to Be the Word of God' and your sermon on 'The Baptism With the Holy Ghost.'"

Time and again, when a call came to me to go off to some church, he would come up to me and say: "Now, Torrey, be sure and preach on the baptism with the Holy Ghost." I do not know how many times he said that to me. Once I asked him: "Mr. Moody, don't you think I have any sermons but those two: 'Ten Reasons Why I Believe the Bible to Be the Word of God' and 'The Baptism With the Holy Ghost?'" "Never mind that," he replied, "you give them those two sermons."

Once he had some teachers at Northfield—fine men, all of them, but they did not believe in a definite baptism with the Holy Ghost for the individual. They believed that every child of God was baptized with the Holy Ghost, and they did not believe in any special baptism with the Holy Ghost for the individual.

Mr. Moody came to me and said: "Torrey, will you come up to my house after the meeting tonight and I will get those men to come, and I want you to talk this thing out with them."

Of course, I very readily consented, and Mr. Moody and I talked for a long time, but they did not altogether see eye to eye with us. And when they went, Mr. Moody signaled me to remain for a few moments. Mr. Moody sat there with his chin on his breast, as he so often sat when he was in deep thought; then he looked up and said: "Oh, why will they split hairs? Why don't they see that this is just the one thing that they themselves need? They are good teachers, they are wonderful teachers, and I am so glad to have them here; but why will they not see that the baptism with the Holy Ghost is just the one touch that they themselves need?"

I shall never forget the eighth of July, 1894, to my dying day. It was the closing day of the Northfield Students' Conference—the gathering of the students from the eastern colleges. Mr. Moody had asked me to preach on Saturday night and Sunday morning on the baptism with the Holy Ghost. On Saturday night I had spoken about, "The Baptism With the Holy Ghost: What It Is; What It Does; the Need of It and the Possibility of It." On Sunday morning I spoke on "The Baptism With the Holy Spirit: How to Get It." It was just exactly twelve o'clock when I finished my morning sermon, and I took out my watch and said: "Mr. Moody has invited us all to go up to the mountain at three o'clock this afternoon to pray for the power of the Holy Spirit. It is three hours to three o'clock. Some of you cannot wait three hours. You do not need to wait. Go to your rooms; go out into the woods; go to your tent; go anywhere where you can get alone with God and have this matter out with Him."

At three o'clock we all gathered in front of Mr. Moody's mother's house (she was then still living), and then began to pass down the lane, through the gate, up on the mountainside. There were four hundred and fifty-six of us in all; I know the number because Paul Moody counted us as we passed through the gate.

After a while Mr. Moody said: "I don't think we need to go any further; let us sit down here." We sat down on stumps and logs and on the ground. Mr. Moody said: "Have any of you students anything to say?" I think about seventy-five of them arose, one after the other, and said: "Mr. Moody, I could not wait till three o'clock; I have been alone with God since the morning service, and I believe I have a right to say that I have been baptized with the Holy Spirit."

When these testimonies were over, Mr. Moody said: "Young men, I can't see any reason why we shouldn't kneel down here right now and ask God that the Holy Ghost may fall upon us just as definitely as He fell upon the apostles on the Day of Pentecost. Let us pray." And we did pray, there on the mountainside. As we had gone up the mountainside heavy clouds had been gathering, and just as we began to pray those clouds broke and the raindrops began to fall through the overhanging pines. But there was another cloud that had been gathering over Northfield for ten days, a cloud big with the mercy and grace and power of God; and as we began to pray our prayers seemed to pierce that cloud and the Holy Ghost fell upon us. Men and women, that is what we all need the Baptism with the Holy Ghost.

Mr. Moody Preaching to Another Great Crowd

A BIOGRAPHICAL SKETCH OF
R.A. TORREY

BY LARRY MARTIN

R. A. Torrey

REUBEN A. TORREY

John R. Rice said probably none of D.L. Moody's associates were as close to the evangelist as R.A. Torrey. He was a colleague and friend. Perhaps no other person would be so well qualified to tell the world the secret to Moody's great power with God.

Even under the shadow of Moody, Torrey excelled as a pastor, evangelist, educator and author. Few men have the genius to reach success in four different areas of ministry.

Torrey was born in Hoboken, New Jersey on January 28, 1856. When he was three the family moved to Brooklyn and then to a large farm in upstate New York. His father was a banker and lawyer and was quite affluent, but through a series of unfortunate events lost his wealth.

Torrey was reared in a Christian home and his mother was a devoted, praying woman. However, his parents were not disciplinarians and Torrey chose the ways of the world.

At the age of 16 he began studies at Yale. His keen intellect made him a model student, but his "free" time was wasted on cards, race tracks and theaters.

A divinely inspired dream led Torrey to conversion in 1875. He surrendered not only to Christ, but to the full-time service. When he graduated from the university, he immediately began ministry preparation at Yale Divinity School. He eventually earned the Doctor of Divinity.

At Yale, Torrey heard D.L. Moody for the first time. Moody's passion for souls was a great inspiration to the young Torrey. During one of his sermons, Moody said, "Faith can do anything!" Those words became the theme of Torrey's life.

Torrey studied in Germany and then became a respected pastor. His life and ministry changed radically in 1889, when Moody tapped him to be the first superintendent of what is now the Moody Bible Institute. Torrey held the position for almost twenty years.

Torrey, a very successful missionary evangelist, held campaigns around the world. Tens of thousands came to Christ under his ministry.

Always an educator, Torrey wrote some forty books on almost all areas of Christian living. In his later years, he conducted Bible conferences and lectured at Moody Bible Institute and in other venues.

Torrey died in Ashville, North Carolina on October 26, 1928. He was seventy-two. One of the speakers at his funeral said, "Those who knew Dr. Torrey more intimately, knew him as a man of regular and uninterrupted prayer. He knew what it meant to pray without ceasing."

Torrey's work for his Master continues through his extensive writings, including *Why God Used D.L. Moody.*

SELECTED SERMONS OF
D.L. MOODY

BY MR. MOODY, HIMSELF

The Many Faces of D. L. Moody
throughout the Stages of a Great Life

THE GATEWAY INTO
THE KINGDOM

*Except a man be born again, he cannot enter the
kingdom of God. John 3:3*

There is no portion of the Word of God, perhaps,
with which we are more familiar than this passage. I suppose if I were to ask those, in any audience if they believed that Jesus Christ taught the doctrine of the new
birth, nine-tenths of them would say: "Yes, I believe He
did."

THE DOCTRINE OF THE NEW BIRTH MOST

IMPORTANT

Now if the words of this text are true they embody
one of the most solemn questions that can come before
us. We can afford to be deceived about many things
rather than about this one thing. Christ makes it very

plain. He says, "Except a man be born again, he cannot *see* the kingdom of God"—much less inherit it. This doctrine of the new birth is therefore the foundation of all our hopes for the world to come. It is really the "A B C" of the Christian religion. My experience has been this—that if a man is unsound on this doctrine he will be unsound on almost every other fundamental doctrine in the Bible. A true understanding of this subject will help a man to solve a thousand difficulties that he may meet with in the Word of God. Things that before seemed very dark and mysterious will become very plain.

The doctrine of the new birth upsets all false religion—all false views about the Bible and about God. A friend of mine once told me that in one of his after-meetings, a man came to him with a long list of questions written out for him to answer. He said: "If you can answer these questions satisfactorily I have made up my mind to become a Christian." "Do you not think," said my friend, "that you had better come to Christ first? Then you can look into these questions." The man thought that perhaps he had better do so. After he had received Christ, he looked again at his list of questions; but then it seemed to him as if they had been answered. Nicodemas came with his troubled mind, and Christ said to him, "Ye must be born again." He was treated altogether differently from what he expected, but I venture to say that was the most blessed night in all his life. To be "born again" is the greatest blessing that will ever come to us in this world.

Notice how the Scripture puts it. "Except a man be born again," "born from above,"* "born of the Spirit." From amongst a number of other passages where we find the word "*except*," I would just name three. "Except ye repent, ye shall all likewise perish" (Luke 13:3,5). "Except ye be converted, and, become as little

---

*John 3:3, marginal reading. Ed.

children, ye shall not enter into the kingdom of heaven" (Matthew 16:3). "Except your, righteousness shall exceed the righteousness of the scribes and Pharisees, ye shall in no case enter into the kingdom of heaven" (Matthew 5:20). They all really mean the same thing.

I am so thankful that our Lord spoke of the new birth to this ruler of the Jews, this doctor of the law, rather than to the woman at the well of Samaria, or Matthew the publican, or to Zaccheus. If he had reserved His teaching on this matter for these three, or such as these, people would have said: "Oh yes, these publicans and harlots need to be converted: but I am an upright man; I do not need to be converted." I suppose Niccodemus was one of the best specimens of the people of Jerusalem: there was nothing on the record against him.

I think it is scarcely necessary for me to prove that we need to be born again before we are meet for heaven. I venture to say that there is no candid man but would say he is not fit for the kingdom of God, until he is born of another spirit. The Bible teaches us that man by nature is lost and guilty, and our experience confirms this. We know also that the best and holiest man, if he turns away from God, will soon fall into sin.

WHAT REGENERATION IS NOT

Now, let me say what regeneration is not. It is not going to church. Very often I see people, and ask them if they are Christians. "Yes, of course I am; at least, I think I am: I go to church every Sunday." Ah, but this is not regeneration. Others say, "I am trying to do what is right—am I not a Christian? Is that not new birth?" No. What has that to do with being born again? There is yet another class—those who have "turned over a new leaf," and they think they are regenerated. No; forming a new resolution is not being born again.

Nor will being baptized do any good. You will hear people say, "Why, I have been baptized; and I was born again when I was baptized." They believe that because they were baptized into the church, they were baptized into the kingdom of God. I tell you it is utterly impossible. You may be baptized into the church, and yet not be baptized into the Son of God. Baptism is all right in its place. God forbid that I should say anything against it. But if you put that in the place of regeneration—in the place of the new birth—it is a terrible mistake. You cannot be baptized into the kingdom of God. "Except a man be *born again*, he cannot see the kingdom of God." If any one reading this rests his hopes on anything else—on any other foundation—I pray that God may sweep it away.

Another class say, "I go to the Lord's Supper; I partake uniformly of the sacrament." Blessed ordinance Jesus hath said that as often as ye do it ye commemorate His death. Yet, that is not being "born again;" that is not passing from death unto life. Jesus says plainly—and so plainly that there need not be any mistake about it—"Except a man be born of the Spirit, he cannot enter into the kingdom of God." What has a sacrament to do with that? What has going to church to do with being born again?

Another man comes up and says, "I say my prayers regularly." Still I say that is not being born of the Spirit. It is a very solemn question, then, that comes up before us; and oh! that every reader would ask himself earnestly and faithfully: "Have I been born again? Have I been born of the Spirit? Have I passed from death unto life?"

WE DO NOT NEED TO BE CONVERTED

There is a class of men who say that special religious meetings are very good for a certain class of people. They would be very good if you could get the drunkard there, or get the gambler there, or get other vicious people there—that would do a great deal of good. But "we do not need to be converted." To whom did Christ utter these words of wisdom? To Nicodemus. Who was Nicodemus? Was he a drunkard, a gambler, or a thief? No! No doubt he was one of the very best men in Jerusalem. He was an honorable councilor; he belonged to the Sanhedrin; he held a very high position; he was an orthodox man; he was one of the very soundest men. And yet what did Christ say to him? "Except a man be born again, he *cannot see* the kingdom of God."

But I can imagine some one saying, "What am I to do? I cannot create life. I certainly cannot save myself." You certainly cannot; and we do not claim that you can. We tell you it is utterly impossible to make a man better without Christ; but that is what men are trying to do. They are trying to patch up this "old Adam" nature. *There must be a new creation.* Regeneration is a new creation; and if it is a new creation it must be the work of God. In the first chapter of Genesis man does not appear. There is no one there but God. Man is not there to take part. When God created the earth He was alone. When Christ redeemed the world He was alone.

"That which is born of the flesh is flesh; and that which is born of the Spirit is spirit" (John 3:6). The Ethiopian cannot change his skin, and the leopard cannot change his spots. You might as well try to make yourselves pure and holy without the help of God. It would be just as easy for you to do that as for the black man to wash himself white. A man might just as well try to leap over the moon as to serve God in the flesh. Therefore, "that which is born of the flesh is flesh; and that which is born of the Spirit is spirit."

HOW TO ENTER INTO THE KINGDOM
OF GOD

Now God tells us in this chapter how we are to get into His kingdom. We are not to work our way in—not but that salvation is worth working for. We admit all that. If there were rivers and mountains in the way, it would be well worth while to swim those rivers, and climb those mountains. There is no doubt that salvation is worth all that effort; but we do not obtain it by our works. It is "to him that worketh not, but believeth" (Romans 4:5). We work because we are saved; we do not work to be saved. We work from the cross; but not towards it. It is written, "Work out your own salvation with fear and trembling" (Philippians 2:12). Why, you must have your salvation before you can work it out. Suppose I say to my little boy, "I want you to spend that hundred dollars carefully." "Well," he says, "let me have the hundred dollars; and I will be careful how I spend it."

I remember when I first left home and went to Boston. I had spent all my money, and I went to the post-office three times a day. I knew there was only one mail a day from home, but I thought by some possibility there might be a letter for me. At last I received a letter from my little sister, and oh, how glad I was to get it. She had heard that there were a great many pickpockets in Boston, and a large part of that letter was to urge me to be very careful not to let anybody pick my pocket. Now I required to have something in my pocket before I could have it picked. So you must have salvation before you can work it out.

When Christ cried out on Calvary, "It is finished!" He meant what He said. All that men have to do now is just to accept of the work of Jesus Christ. There is no hope for man or woman so long as they are trying to work out salvation for themselves. I can imagine there are some people who will say as Nicodemus possibly did: "This is a very mysterious thing." I see the scowl on that Pharisee's brow as he says: "How can these things be?" It sounds very strange to his ear. "Born again; born of the Spirit! How can these things be?" A great many people say: "You must reason it out; but if you do not reason it out, do not ask us to believe it." I can imagine a great many people saying that. When you ask me to reason it out, I tell you frankly I cannot do it. "The wind bloweth where it listeth, and thou hearest the sound thereof, but canst not tell whence it cometh, and whither it goeth; so is every one that is born of the Spirit" (John 3:8). I do not understand everything about the wind. You ask me to reason it out. I cannot. It may blow due north here, and a hundred miles away due south. I may go up a few hundred feet, and find it blowing in an entirely opposite direction from what it is down here. You ask me to explain these currents of wind; but suppose that, because I cannot explain them, and do not understand them, I were to take my stand and assert, "Oh, there is no such thing as wind." I can imagine some little girl saying: "I know more about it than that man does; often have I heard the wind, and felt it blowing against my face;" and she might say: "Did not the wind blow my umbrella out of my hands the other day? and did I not see it blow a man's hat off in the street? Have I not, seen it blow the trees in the forest, and the growing corn in the country?"

You might just as well tell me that there is no such thing as wind as tell me there is no such thing as a man being born of the Spirit. I have felt the Spirit of God working in my heart, just as really and as truly as I have felt the wind blowing in my face. I cannot reason it out. There are a great many things I cannot reason out, but which I believe. I never could reason out the creation. I can see the world, but I cannot tell how God made it out of nothing. But almost every man will admit there was a creative power.

IMPOSSIBLE TO EXPLAIN EVERYTHING

There are a great many things that I cannot explain and cannot reason out, and yet that I believe. I heard a commercial traveler say that he had heard that the ministry and religion of Jesus Christ were matters of revelation and not of investigation. "When it pleased God to reveal His Son in me," says Paul (Galatians 1:15, 16). There was a party of young men together, going up the country; and on their journey they made up their minds not to believe anything they could not reason out. An old man heard them, and presently he said: "I heard you say you would not believe anything you could not reason out." "Yes," they said, "that is so." "Well," he said, "coming down on the train today, I noticed some geese, some sheep, some swine, and some cattle all eating grass. Can you tell me by what process that same grass was turned into hair, feathers, bristles and wool? Do you believe it is a fact?" "Oh yes," they said, "we cannot help believing that, though we fail to understand it." "Well," said the old man, "I cannot help believing in Jesus Christ." And I cannot help believing in the regeneration of man, when I see men who have been reclaimed, when I see men who have been reformed. Have not some of, the very worst men been regenerated—been picked up out of the pit, and had their feet set upon the Rock, and a new song put in their mouths? Their tongues were cursing and blaspheming, and now are occupied in praising God. Old things have passed away, and all things have become new. They are not reformed only, but *regenerated*—new men in Christ Jesus.

PRACTICAL RESULTS IN REAL LIFE

Down there in the dark alleys of one of our great cities is a poor drunkard. I think if you want to get near hell, you should go to a poor drunkard's home. Go to the house of that poor miserable drunkard. Is there anything more like hell on earth? See the want and distress that reign there. But hark! A footstep is heard at the door, and the children run and hide themselves. The patient wife waits to meet the man. He has been her torment. Many a time she has borne about the marks of his blows for weeks. Many a time that strong right hand has been brought down on her defenseless head. And now she waits expecting to hear his oaths and suffer his brutal treatment. He comes in and says to her: "I have been to the meeting; and I heard there that if I will I can be converted. I believe that God is able to save me." Go down to that house again in a few weeks: and what a change! As you approach you hear some one singing. It is, not the song of a reveller, but the strains of that good old hymn, "Rock of Ages." The children are no longer afraid of the man but cluster around his knee. His wife is near him, her face lit up with a happy glow. Is not that a picture of regeneration? I can take you to many such homes, made happy by the regenerating power of the religion of Christ. What men want is the power to overcome temptation, the power to lead a right life.

The only way to get into the kingdom of God is to be "born" into it. The law of this country requires that the president should be born in this country. When, foreigners come to our shores they have no right to complain against such a law, which forbids them from ever becoming presidents. Now, has not God a right to make a law that all those who become heirs of eternal life must be "born" into His kingdom?

An unregenerated man would rather be in hell than in heaven. Take a man whose heart is full of corruption and wickedness, and place him in heaven among the pure, the holy and the redeemed; and he would not want to stay there. Certainly, if we are to be happy in heaven we must begin, to make a heaven here on earth. Heaven is a prepared place for a prepared people. If a gambler or a blasphemer were taken out of the streets of New York and placed on the crystal pavement of heaven and under the shadow of the tree of life, he would say, "I do not want to stay here." If men were taken to heaven just as they are by nature, without having their hearts regenerated, there would be another rebellion in heaven. Heaven is filled with a company of those who have been *twice born.*

In the fourteenth and fifteenth verses of this chapter we read "As Moses lifted up the serpent in the wilderness, even so must the Son of Man be lifted up: that whosoever believeth in Him should not perish, but have eternal life."

WHOSOEVER

Mark that! Let me tell you who are unsaved what God has done for you. He has done everything that He could do toward your salvation. You need not wait for God to do anything more. In one place He asks the question, what more could He have done (Isaiah 5:4). He sent

His prophets, and they killed them; then He sent His beloved Son, and they murdered Him. Now He has sent the Holy Spirit to convince us of sin, and to show how we are to be saved.

In this chapter we are told how men are to be saved, namely, by Him who was lifted up on the cross. Just as Moses lifted up the brazen serpent in the wilderness, so must the Son of Man be lifted up, "that whosoever believeth in Him should not perish, but have eternal life." Some men complain and say that it is very unreasonable that they should be held responsible for the sin of a man six thousand years ago. It was not long ago that a man was talking to me about this injustice, as he called it. If a man thinks he is going to answer God in that way, I tell you it will not do him any good. If you are lost, it will not be on account of Adam's sin.

THE CASE ILLUSTRATED

Let me illustrate this, and perhaps you will be better able to understand it. Suppose I am dying of consumption, which I inherited from my father or mother. I did not get the disease by any fault of my own, by any neglect of my health; I inherited it, let us suppose. A friend happens to come along, he looks at me, and says: "Moody, you have consumption." I reply, "I know it very well; I do not want any one to tell me that." "But," he says, "there is a remedy." "But, sir, I do not believe it. I have tried the leading physicians in this country and in Europe; and they tell me there is no hope." "But you know me, Moody; you have known me for years." "Yes, sir." "Do you think, then, I would tell you a falsehood?" "No." "Well, ten years ago I was as far gone. I was given up by the physicians to die, but I took this medicine and it cured me. I am perfectly well; look at me." I say that it is "a very strange case." "Yes, it may be strange;

but it is a fact. This medicine cured me. Take this medicine, and it will cure you. Although it has cost me a great deal, it shall not cost you anything. Do not make light of it, I beg of you." "Well," I say, "I should like to believe you; but this is contrary to my reason."

Hearing this, my friend goes away and returns with another friend, and that one testifies to the same thing. I am still disbelieving; so he goes away, and brings in another friend, and another, and another, and another; and they all testify to the same thing. They say they were as bad as myself; that they took the same medicine that has been offered to me; and that it has cured them. My friend then hands me the medicine. I dash it to the ground; I do not believe in its saving power; I die. The reason is then that I spurned the remedy. So, if you perish, it will not be because Adam fell, but because you spurned the remedy offered to save you. You will choose darkness rather than light. "How then shall we escape, if we neglect so great salvation?" There is no hope for you if you neglect the remedy. It does no good to look at the wound. If we had been in the Israelitish camp and had been bitten by one of the fiery serpents, it would have done us no good to look at the wound. Looking at the wound will never save any one. What you must do is to look at the Remedy—look away to Him who hath power to save you from your sin.

Behold the camp of the Israelites; look at the scene that is pictured to your eyes. Many are dying because they neglect the remedy that is offered. In that arid desert is many a short and tiny grave; many a child has been bitten by the fiery serpents. Fathers and mothers are bearing away their children. Over yonder they are just burying a mother; a loved mother is about to be laid in the earth. All the family weeping, gather around the beloved form. You hear the mournful cries;

you see the bitter tears. The father is being borne away to his last resting place. There is wailing going up all over the camp. Tears are pouring down for thousands who have passed away; thousands more are dying; and the plague is raging from one end of the camp to the other.

LIFE IN A LOOK

I see in one tent an Israelitish mother bending over the form of a beloved boy just coming into the bloom of life, just budding into manhood. She is wiping away the sweat of death that is gathering upon his brow. Yet a little while, and his eyes are fixed and glassy, for life is ebbing fast away. The mother's heart-strings are torn and bleeding. All at once she hears a noise in the camp. A great shout goes up. What does it mean? She goes to the door of the tent. "What is the noise in the camp?" she asks those passing by. And some one says: "Why, my good woman, have you not heard the good news that has come into the camp?" "No," says the woman, "Good news! What is it?" "Why, have you not heard about it?" "God his provided a remedy." "What! for the bitten Israelites? Oh, tell me what the remedy is!" "Why, God has instructed Moses to make a brazen serpent, and to put it on a pole in the middle of the camp; and He has declared that whosoever looks upon it shall live. The shout that you hear is the shout of the people when they see, the serpent lifted up."

The mother goes back into the tent, and she says: "My boy, I have good news to tell you. You need not die! My boy, my boy, I have come with good tidings; you can live!" He is already getting stupified; he is so weak he cannot walk to the door of the tent. She puts her strong arms under him and lifts him up. "Look yonder; look right there under the hill!" But the boy does not see anything. He says: "I do not see anything; what is it, mother?" And she says: "Keep looking, and you will see it." At last he catches a glimpse of the glistening serpent; and lo, he is well! And thus it is with many a young convert. Some men say: "Oh, we do not believe in sudden conversions." How long did it take to cure that boy? How long did it take to cure those serpent-bitten Israelites? It was just a look, and they were well.

That Hebrew boy is a young convert. I can fancy that I see him now calling on all those who were with him to praise God. He sees another young man bitten as he was, and he runs up to him and tells him, "You need not die." "Oh," the young man replies, "I cannot live; it is not possible. There is not a physician in Israel who can cure me." He does not know that he need not die. "Why, have you not heard the news? God has provided a remedy." "What remedy?" "Why, God has told Moses to lift up a brazen serpent, and has said that none of those who look upon that serpent shall die." I can just imagine the young man. He may be what you call an intellectual young man. He says to the young convert: "You do not think I am going to believe anything like that? If the physicians in Israel cannot cure me, how do you think that an old brass serpent on a pole is going to cure me?" "Why, sir, I was as bad as yourself!" "You do not say so!" "Yes, I do." "That is the most astonishing thing I ever heard," says the young man: "I wish you would explain the philosophy of it." "I cannot. I only know that I looked at that serpent, and I was cured: that did it."

I JUST LOOKED; THAT IS ALL

"My mother told me the reports that were being heard through the camp; and I just believed what my mother said, and I am perfectly well." "Well, I do not believe you were bitten as badly as I have been." The young man pulls up his sleeve. "Look there! That mark shows where I was bitten; and I tell you I was worse than you are!" "Well, if I understood the philosophy of it I would look and get well." "Let your philosophy go; *look and live!*" "But, sir you ask me to do an unreasonable thing. If God had said, Take the brass and rub it into the wound, there might be something in the brass that would cure the bite. Young man, explain the philosophy of it." I have often seen people before me who have talked in that way. But the young man calls in another, and takes him into the tent, and says: "Just tell him how the Lord saved you;" and he tells just the same story; and he calls in others, and they all say the same thing.

The young man says it is a very strange thing, "If the Lord had told Moses to go and get some herbs, or roots, and stew them, and take the decoction as a medicine, there would be something in that. But it is so contrary to nature to do such a thing as look at the serpent, that I cannot do it." At length his mother, who has been out in the camp, comes in, and she says, "My boy, I have just the best news in the world for you. I was in the camp, and I saw hundreds who were very far gone, and they are all perfectly well now." The young man says: "I should like to get well; it is a very painful thought to die; I want to go into the promised land, and it is terrible to die here in this wilderness; but the fact is—I do not understand the remedy. It does not appeal to my reason. I cannot believe that I can get well in a moment." And the young man dies in consequence of his own unbelief.

GOD'S REMEDY FOR SIN

God provided a remedy for this bitten Israelite— "Look and live!" And there is eternal life for every poor sinner. Look, and you can be saved, my reader, this very hour. God has provided a remedy; and it is offered to all. The trouble is, a great many people are looking at the pole. Do not look at the pole; that is the church. You need not look at the church; the church is all right, but the church cannot save you. Look beyond the pole. Look at the Crucified One. Look to Calvary. Bear in mind, sinner, that Jesus died for all. You need not look at ministers; they are just God's chosen instruments to hold up the Remedy, to hold up Christ. And so, my friend, take your eyes off from men; take your eyes off from the church. Lift them up to Jesus, who took away the sin of the world, and there will be life for you from this hour.

Thank God, we do not require an education to teach us how to look. That little girl, that little boy, only four years old, who cannot read, can look. When the father is coming home, the mother says to her little boy, "Look! look! look!" and the little child learns to look long before he is a year old. And that is the way to be saved. It is to look at the Lamb of God "who taketh away the sin of the world;" and there is life this moment for every one who is willing to look.

HOW TO BE SAVED

Some men say: "I wish I knew how to be saved." Just take God at His word, and trust His Son this very day—this very hour—this very moment. He will save you, if you will trust Him. I imagine I hear some one saying: "I do not feel the bite as much as I wish I did. I know I am a sinner, and all that; but I do not feel the bite enough." How much does God want you to feel it?

When I was in Belfast I knew a doctor who had a friend, a leading surgeon there; and he told me that the surgeon's custom was, before performing any operation, to say to the patient, "Take a good look at the wound, and then fix your eyes on me; and do not take them off till I get through." I thought at the time that was a good illustration. Sinner, take a good look at your wound; and then fix your eyes on Christ, and do not take them off. It is better to look at the Remedy than at the wound. See what a poor wretched sinner you are; and then look at the Lamb of God who "taketh away the sin of the world." He died for the ungodly and the sinner. Say, "I will take Him!" And may God help you to lift your eye to the Man on Calvary. And as the Israelites looked upon the serpent and were healed, so may you look and live.

THE DYING SOLDIER

After the battle of Pittsburgh Landing I was in a hospital at Murfreesboro. In the middle of the night I was aroused and told that a man in one of the wards wanted to see me. I went to him and he called me "chaplain"—I was not the chaplain—and said he wanted me to help him die. And I said, "I would take you right up in my arms and carry you into the kingdom of God, if I could, but I cannot do it. I cannot help you die!" And he said, "Who can?" I said, "The Lord Jesus Christ can—He came for that purpose." He shook his head, and said: "He cannot save me; I have sinned all my life." And I said, "But He came to save sinners." I thought of his mother in the north, and I was sure that she was anxious that he should die in peace; so I resolved I would stay with him. I prayed two or three times, and repeated all the promises I could; for it was evident that in a few hours he would be gone.

I said I wanted to read him a conversation that Christ had with a man who was anxious about his soul. I turned to the third chapter of John. His eyes were riveted on me; and when I came to the fourteenth and fifteenth verses—the passage before us—he caught up the words, "As Moses lifted up the serpent in the wilderness, even so must the Son of Man be lifted up; that whosoever believeth in Him should not perish, but have eternal life." He stopped me and said: "Is that there?" I said, "Yes." He asked me to read it again; and I did so. He leaned his elbows on the cot and clasping his hands together, said: "That's good; won't you read it again?" I read it the third time; and then went on with the rest of the chapter. When I had finished, his eyes were closed, his hands were folded, and there was a smile on his face. Oh, how it was lit up! What a change had come over it! I saw his lips quivering, and, leaning over him, I heard in a faint whisper, "As Moses lifted up the serpent in the wilderness, even so must the Son of Man be lifted up that whosoever believeth in Him should not perish, but have eternal life." He opened his eyes and said: "That's enough; don't read any more." He lingered a few hours, pillowing his head on those two verses; and then went up in one of Christ's chariots, to take his seat in the kingdom of God.

Christ said to Nicodemus: "Except a man be born again, he cannot see the kingdom of God." You may see many countries; but there is one country—the land of Beulah, which John Bunyan saw in vision—you shall never behold, unless you are born again—regenerated by Christ. You can look abroad and see many beautiful trees; but the tree of life, you shall never behold, unless your eyes are made clear by faith in the Savior. You may see the beautiful rivers of the earth—you may ride upon their bosoms; but bear in mind that your eye will never rest upon the river which bursts out from the throne of God and flows through the upper kingdom, unless you are born again. God has said it, and not man. You will never see the kingdom of God except you are born again. You may see the kings and lords of the earth, but the King of kings and Lord of lords you will never see except you are born again. When you are in London you may go to the Tower and see the crown of England, which is worth thousands of dollars, and is guarded there by soldiers; but bear in mind that your eye will never rest upon the crown of life except you are born again.

WHAT THOSE NOT BORN AGAIN SHALL MISS

You may hear the songs of Zion which are sung here; but one song—that of Moses and the Lamb—the uncircumcised ear shall never hear; its melody will only gladden the ear of those who have been born again. You may look upon the beautiful mansions of earth, but bear in mind the mansions which Christ has gone to prepare you shall never see, unless you are born again. It is God who says it. You may see ten thousand beautiful things in this world; but the city that Abraham caught a glimpse of and from that time became a pilgrim and sojourner—you shall never see, unless you are born again (Hebrews 11:8, 10-16). You may often be invited to marriage feasts here; but you will never attend the marriage supper of the Lamb, except you are born again. It is God who says it, dear friend. You may be looking on the face of your sainted mother tonight, and feel that she is praying for you; but the time will come when you shall never see her more, unless you are born again.

A PROMISE MADE TO MOTHER

The reader may be a young man or a young lady who has recently stood by the bedside of a dying mother;

and she may have said: "Be sure and meet me in heaven," and you made the promise. Ah! you shall never see her more, except you are born again. I believe Jesus of Nazareth, sooner than those infidels who say you do not need to be born again. Parents, if you hope to see your children who have gone before, you must be born of the Spirit. Possibly you are a father or mother who has recently borne a loved one to the grave; and how dark your home seems! Never more will you see your child, unless you are born again. If you wish to be reunited to your loved one, you must be born again.

I may be addressing a father or a mother who has a loved one up yonder. If you could hear that loved one's voice, it would say, "Come this way." Have you a sainted friend up yonder? Young man or young lady, have you not a mother in the world of light? If you could hear her speak, would not she say, "Come this way, my son,"— "Come this way, my daughter?" If you would ever see her more you must be born again.

We all have an Elder Brother there. Nearly nineteen hundred years ago He crossed over, and from the heavenly shores He is calling you to heaven. Let us turn our backs upon the world. Let us give a deaf ear to the world. Let us look to Jesus on the cross, and be saved. Then we shall one day see the King in His beauty, and we shall go no more out.

From *The Way to God*, 1884.

BE NOT DECEIVED: GOD IS NOT MOCKED

"Let no man deceive you." Ephesians 5:6

"As one man mocketh another, do ye so mock Him?"
Job 13:9

We have all lived long enough to know what it is to be deceived. We have been deceived by our friends, by our enemies, our neighbors, our relatives. Ungodly companions have deceived us. At every turn of life we have been imposed upon in one way or another.

False teachers have crossed our path, and under pretence of doing us good, have poisoned our mind with error. They have held out hopes to us that have proved false; apples of Sodom, fair without, but full of ashes within. They have told us that there is no God, no future life, no judgment to come; or they have said that all men will be saved, that there is ample time to repent, that we may be saved by doing the best we can.

Sin has deceived us. Every sinner is under a delusion. Sin meets him smilingly and holds out to him pleasures and delights that are not pure and lasting.

During our meetings in Boston a young man came into the Tabernacle. He looked around and he thought to himself the people that came there were great fools—those who had business, and comfortable homes, and good clothes. He had nothing in the world—he was a tramp, and went in there to keep himself warm. But to think that people who had homes would come and spend their time in listening to such stuff as I preached was more than he could understand.

One night after he had been coming there for two weeks, I happened to point right down where he was sitting, and I said, "Young man, be not deceived!" God used that as an arrow. He began to think about himself. His mind went back to the time when he had a good situation in Boston; when he was a young man getting a good salary; when he was in good society and had a great many friends.

Then he looked at his present condition. His friends were all gone, his clothes were gone, his money was gone; and there he was, an outcast in that city. He said to himself, "I have been deceived," and that very hour God waked him. He wanted to get friends to pray for him; but as he was not able to buy a piece of paper, or pay for a postage stamp, he got an old piece of soiled paper, stood up in the street, and wrote a request to be read in the Tabernacle, that if God would save a poor, lost man like him, he wanted to be saved. That prayer was answered. As in the case of

Nebuchadnezzar, his friends gathered around him again, and the Lord restored him to position and to society. His eyes were opened to see how he had been deceived.

SATAN

How many men all over the world are being deceived by the god of this world! It has been asserted that during the late Franco-German war, German drummers and trumpeters used to give the French beats and calls in order to deceive their enemies. The command to "halt," or "cease firing," was often given by the Germans, it has been said, and the French soldiers were thus placed in positions where they could be shot down like cattle.

Satan is the arch-enemy of our souls, and he has often blinded our reason and deceived our conscience by his falsehoods. He has often come as an angel of light, concealing his hideousness under a borrowed cloak. He says to a young man: "Sow your wild oats. Time enough to be religious when you grow old." The young man yields himself to a life of extravagance and excess, under the false hope that he will obtain solid satisfaction; and it is well if he awakens to the deception before his appetites become tyrants, dragging him down into depths of want and woe. Satan promises great things to his victims in the indulgence of their lusts, but they never realize the promises. The promised pleasure turns out to be pain, the promised heaven a hell.

Beware lest Satan deceive you as he deceived Eve in the beginning. There is no truth in him. When he speaketh a lie, he speaketh of his own, for he is a liar, and the father of it."

OUR HEART

But we have been deceived by our own heart most of all. Who has not proved the truth of the Scripture: "The heart is deceitful above all things and desperately wicked; who can know it?" How many times we have said that we never would do a certain thing again, and then have done it within twenty-four hours! A man may think he has fathomed its depths, but he finds there are further depths he has not reached. What gross self-deception is due to it! "He that trusteth in his own heart is a fool," said Solomon. Luther once said he feared his own heart more than the Pope and all the cardinals.

Many a weeping wife has come to me about her husband, saying: "He is good at heart." The truth is— that is the worst spot in him. If the heart was good, all else would be right. Out of the heart are the issues of life. Christ said: "From within, out of the heart of men, proceed evil thoughts, adulteries, fornications, murders, thefts, covetousness, wickedness, deceit, lasciviousness, an evil eye, blasphemy, pride, foolishness." That is Christ's own statement regarding the unregenerate heart.

Some years ago a remarkable picture was exhibited in London. As you looked at it from a distance, you seemed to see a monk engaged in prayer, his hands clasped, his head bowed. As you came nearer, however, and examined the painting more closely, you saw that in reality he was squeezing a lemon into a punch bowl!

What a picture that is of the human heart! Superficially examined, it is thought to be the seat of all that is good and noble and pleasing in a man; whereas in reality, until regenerated by the Holy Ghost, it is the seat of all corruption. "This is the condemnation, that light is come into the world, and men *loved darkness rather than light.*"

A Jewish rabbi once asked his scholars what was the best thing a man could have in order to keep him in the straight path. One said *a good disposition;* another, *a good companion;* another said *wisdom* was the best thing he could desire. At last a scholar replied that he thought *a good heart* was best of all.

"True," said the rabbi, "you have comprehended all that the others have said. For he that hath a good heart will be of a good disposition, and a good companion, and a wise man. Let every one, therefore, cultivate a sincerity and uprightness of heart at all times, and it will save him an abundance of sorrow." We need to make the prayer of David—"Create in me a clean heart, O God, and renew a right spirit within me!"

GOD IS NOT MOCKED

Bear in mind, the God of the Bible has never deceived anyone, and never can, and never will; that is the difference between the God of the Bible and the god of this world. He beholds the ways of men; He looks into their hearts; He knows their secret ways; they need not tell Him or try to conceal anything from Him.

However successfully we may deceive or be deceived by ourselves or others, we cannot deceive Him. Adam and Eve tried it in Eden when they hid themselves from the presence of Jehovah amongst the trees of the garden. Saul tried it when he spared the best of the sheep and oxen of the Amalekites under the pretence of sacrificing them to God. Ananias and Sapphira tried it when they kept back part of the price of the land they sold. "Why hath Satan filled thine heart to lie unto (deceive) the Holy Ghost ? . . . Thou hast not lied unto men, but unto God."

Men try it every day. They have got it into their heads that God can be mocked. Because they can deceive their pastor, and their employer, and their friends, they think they can deceive God. They put on false appearances, they use empty words, they perform unreal service, they make idle excuses, they indulge in all kinds of hypocrisy. But it is of no avail. God cannot be imposed upon. He sees the corruption inside the whited sepulchre.

WARNING TO CHRISTIANS

It is worth noticing that this warning was given by Paul to Christian men—converts in the Galatian church. After all, a man is not all the time deceived about the grosser sins. The drunkard realizes in his sober moments what must be the end of a course of intemperance. Loss of self-respect and of the esteem of friends, the marks he soon begins to bear in his body—unsteady hands and discolored features—these things are the quick harvest of drunkenness, and may easily be detected as they ripen. The licentious man, also, reaps the early fruit of his sin in diseases of the body, which are often effective warnings against continuing in such a dangerous path. But with "respectable" sins it is different. A man may be sowing for years, and not even realize it himself.

You remember that in the parable of the sower some seeds fell among thorns, and the thorns sprung up and choked them. Our Master, expounding this parable, said: "He that received seed among the thorns is he that heareth the word: but *the care of this world and the deceitfulness of riches* choke the word, and he becometh unfruitful." Who would have expected this result of the world or of riches? But it has been said that Christ never spoke of riches except in words of warning. We are not apt to regard them in that light today. Men are trampling each other down in the pursuit of wealth. "Be not deceived." He who sets his heart upon money is sowing to the flesh, and shall of the flesh reap corruption. "Adversity hath slain her thousands, but prosperity her tens of thousands."

"What is the value of this estate?" said a gentleman to another, as they passed a fine mansion surrounded by fair and fertile fields.

"I don't know what it is valued at; I know what it cost its late possessor."

"How much?"

"His soul."

An English clergyman was called to the deathbed of a wealthy parishioner. Kneeling beside the dying man the pastor asked him to take his hand as he prayed for his upholding in that solemn hour, but he declined to give it. After the end had come, and they turned down the coverlet, the rigid hands were found holding the safe key in their death grip. Heart and hand, to the last, clinging to his possessions, but he could not take them with him.

A man may be proud, and his very sin reckoned a virtue. Hear what the Word of God says: "Haughtiness of eyes and a proud heart is *sin;*" "every one that is proud in heart is an abomination to the Lord."

These are the mistakes men make. They are leading respectable lives, and they think that all is well. They do not recognize the taint of corruption upon many of the most cherished objects of their hearts. Christian professors, most of all, need to beware lest they are being deceived.

NEGLECT

How watchful men should be of their thoughts, their practices, their feelings! The reason of deception is, for the most part, neglect. Men do not stop to examine themselves, to lay their hearts and minds bare as in the sight of God, and judge themselves by His most holy will. A man need not shoot himself in order to commit suicide: he need only neglect the proper means of sustenance, and he will soon die. Where an enemy is strong and aggressive, an army is doomed to sure defeat and capture unless a sharp lookout is kept, every man wide awake at his post of duty.

It has been noticed that there are more accidents in Switzerland in fine seasons than in stormy ones. People are apt to undertake expeditions that they would not take under less favorable conditions, and they are less careful in their conduct. And so it is that moral and spiritual disaster usually overtakes men when they are off their guard, careless against temptation. They become proud and self-reliant in seasons of prosperity, whereas adversity drives them to the living God for guidance and comfort.

Dr. Johnson once said that it is more from carelessness, regarding the truth than from intentional lying that there is so much falsehood in the world.

Hence, the necessity of continual watchfulness. The Persians had an annual festival when they slew all the serpents and venomous creatures they could find; but they allowed them to swarm as fast and freely as ever until the festival came round once more. It was poor policy Sins, like serpents, breed quickly and need to be constantly watched.

And we ought to watch on every side. Many a man has fallen at the very point where he thought he was safest. The meekness of Moses has passed into a proverb. Yet he lost the Promised Land, because he allowed the children of Israel to provoke him, and "he spake unadvisedly with his lips." Peter was the most zealous and defiant of the disciples, bold and outspoken; yet he degenerated for a short time into a lying, swearing, sneaking coward, afraid of a maid.

There is an old fable that a doe that had but one eye used to graze near the sea; and in order to be safe, she kept her blind eye toward the water, from which side she expected no danger, while with the good eye she watched the country. Some men, perceiving this, took a boat and came upon her from the sea and shot her. With her dying breath, she said: "Oh! Hard fate! That I should receive my death wound from that side whence I expected no harm, and be safe in the part where I looked for most danger."

Let danger and need drive you closer to God. He never slumbers or sleeps, and in His keeping you will be safe, seize hold of Him in prayer. Watch and pray.

CHRISTIANITY NOT RESPONSIBLE

Christianity is not responsible for the deception that exists among its professing disciples. The illustration has been used before that you might just as reasonably hold the Cunard company* responsible for the suicide of a passenger who jumps overboard one of their vessels at sea. Had the person remained on the vessel,

---

*A popular cruise line. Ed.

he would have been safe, and had the disciple remained true to his principles, he would never have turned out a hypocrite. Was anybody ever more severe in denouncing hypocrisy than Christ? Do you want to know the reason why, every now and then, the church is scandalized by the exposure of some leading church member or Sabbath school superintendent? It is not his Christianity, but his lack of it. Some secret sin has been eating at the heart of the tree, and in a critical moment it is blown down and its rottenness revealed.

THE DECEPTION CANNOT LAST FOREVER

It is impossible for the deception to last forever. Lincoln had a saying that you may be able to deceive all the people some of the time, and some of the people all of the time, but you will not be able to deceive all the people all of the time. Death will uncover the deception, if it has not been detected sooner; and the unfortunate victim will stand, undeceived, in the presence of a God who cannot be mocked.

From *Sowing and Reaping*, 1896.

THE APOSTOLIC FAITH

Pentecost Has Come

Los Angeles Being Visited by a Revival of Bible Salvation and Pentecost as Recorded in the Book of Acts

The Comforter Has Come!

WWW.AZUSASTREET.ORG

Ask Your Christian Bookstore to Stock these Great Books on Revival.

The Great Revival in Wales

Other Great Books for your *REVIVAL* Library

CHRISTIAN LIFE BOOKS

P.O. BOX 5
DUNCAN, OKLAHOMA 73534
www.rrmi.org & www.azusastreet.org
info@azusastreet.org

Made in the USA
Coppell, TX
19 September 2025

54808056R00056